BECOME A
○ FOSSIL ○
EXPLORER

THE GREAT BIG
BOOK OF
DINOSAURS

QED

QED Publishing

Rupert
Matthews

CONTENTS

COMBAT

DINO GUIDE

Words in **bold** can be found in the glossary on page 113.

DINOSAUR DIG

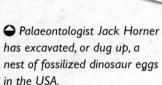

Palaeontologist Jack Horner has excavated, or dug up, a nest of fossilized dinosaur eggs in the USA.

Dinosaurs **were** reptiles **that lived on Earth. They became** extinct **about 65 million years ago. There are no dinosaurs alive today.**

Scientists called **palaeontologists** (pay-lee-on-toll-oh-jists) study dinosaurs. By examining dinosaur remains, called **fossils**, palaeontologists can show what dinosaurs looked like when they were alive.

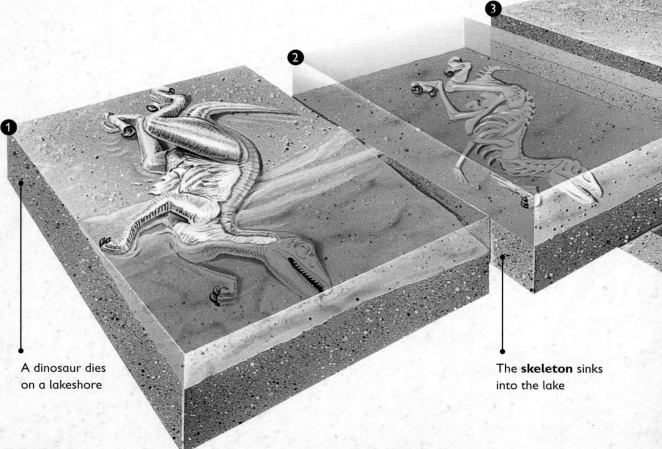

1 A dinosaur dies on a lakeshore

2

3

The **skeleton** sinks into the lake

Many dinosaur remains have been found – of all different types from several different times. These remains help palaeontologists to understand how these creatures lived and behaved.

⬤ *When a plant or animal dies, it usually rots away completely. However, in special conditions, parts of it can become fossilized.*

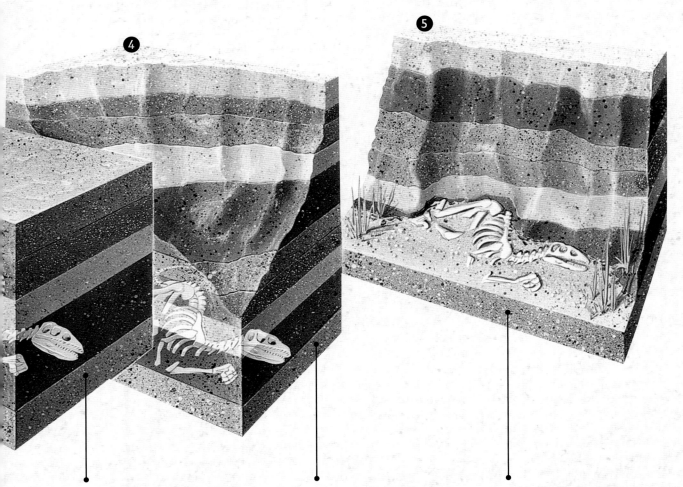

Layers of mud settle over the skeleton. The mud and bones gradually turn into stone

The rock wears away, or **erodes**

As more rock erodes, the skeleton is revealed

FAMILIES

Did you know that eggs were
hatched in nurseries?

Or that some dinosaurs lived in
herds and some alone?

Read on to discover everything you need to
know about dinosaur families…

CARING FOR THE EGGS

Dinosaurs laid eggs, which were kept warm and safe until they hatched **into babies.**

In hot areas, the eggs were laid on the warm ground. The mother dinosaur would stay nearby to provide shade from the sun if the eggs became too hot.

In cooler parts of the world, the mother dinosaur may have piled leaves on top of the eggs. As the leaves rotted, they produced heat, which kept the eggs warm.

DINOSAUR DIG
Jobaria

WHERE: Niger, Africa

PERIOD: 110 million years ago in the early Cretaceous

DIG SITE

WOW!

In July 1923, Roy Chapman Andrews and his team found the first dinosaur eggs in Mongolia, Asia – they were *Oviraptor* (oh-vee-rap-tor) eggs.

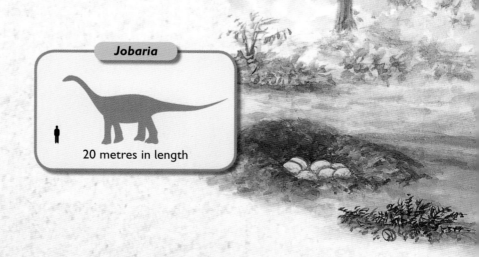

Jobaria

20 metres in length

◐ This model shows a baby dinosaur inside its egg. The baby feeds on the sac, or bag, of orange yolk. It breathes the oxygen that filters through the egg shell.

◐ A mother Jobaria (joe-barr-ee-ah) tries to drive off a smaller hunting dinosaur. Many dinosaur eggs were eaten before they had a chance to hatch.

THE NURSERY

Some dinosaurs built large nurseries **where more than 100 dinosaurs laid their eggs in nests close to each other.**

After the eggs hatched, the adult dinosaurs brought food to their young and guarded the nursery from attack. The babies stayed in the nest for several weeks.

Hunting dinosaurs may have cared for their babies in a similar way. Young hunters probably followed their parents for several months so that they could learn how to hunt successfully.

DINOSAUR DIG
Maiasaura

WHERE: Montana, North America

PERIOD: 75 million years ago in the late Cretaceous

DIG SITE

◐ Maiasaura (my-yah-saw-rah) would hatch from their eggs after eight to ten weeks.

The young Maiasaura stayed in the nursery for several weeks after they hatched, so they could be cared for by their parents.

Maiasaura

9 metres in length

YOUNGSTERS

Young animals, including dinosaurs, look and behave differently from adults.

Their head and eyes are large in proportion to their body – this makes their body look too small! Their legs tend to be shorter and thicker than those of adults.

Mussaurus (muss-saw-rus) had a large head, large eyes and short legs. Scientists think that the fossil they have found is of a baby animal. The adult would have been much larger and looked different.

DIG SITE

◗ *A baby Mussaurus would only have been 20 centimetres in length – about the size of a rat.*

WOW!

Fossils of a young *Tyrannosaurus* (tie-rann-oh-saw-rus) have been found. The remains show that it was probably a fierce killer, just like the adult.

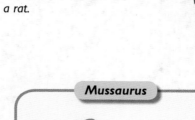

Mussaurus

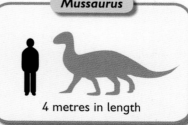

4 metres in length

● *The fossil of Mussaurus is one of the smallest dinosaur skeletons ever found, but it is of a baby. The adult would have been about 4 metres in length.*

LEAVING THE NEST

Not all dinosaurs cared for their young in nurseries. Some youngsters had to look after themselves.

Young **sauropods**, such as *Apatosaurus* (ap-at-oh-saw-rus), hid from hunters in bushes and other **undergrowth**. As they grew larger, the youngsters may have left the safety of cover as they were able to fight off attackers.

Fossil footprints show that sauropods waded into lakes or rivers. They may have been hiding or escaping from hunters.

DINOSAUR DIG
Apatosaurus

WHERE: Wyoming, North America

PERIOD: 150 million years ago in the late Jurassic

DIG SITE

Apatosaurus

25 metres in length

● Young sauropods, such as Apatosaurus, left the nest when they were only a few days old. Adults collected soft plants for the babies to eat when they hatched, but then they ignored their young.

WOW!

Fossils of *Apatosaurus* came from rocks of the Morrison Formation, USA. These contain more dinosaur fossils than any other rocks on Earth.

15

Some scientists believe that baby dinosaurs sometimes followed their parents instead of living by themselves.

A young dinosaur relied on its parent for protection against attack. The youngster would have learned many skills by watching its parent, including which plants were good to eat, which food to avoid, and which dinosaurs were dangerous hunters.

DINOSAUR DIG
Cetiosaurus

WHERE: England, Europe

PERIOD: 180 million years ago in the mid Jurassic

DIG SITE

WOW!

In 1868, a complete Cetiosaurus skeleton was discovered by English palaeontologist, Sir Richard Owen.

◗ *The backbone of Cetiosaurus (set-ee-oh-saw-rus) looks similar to a whale's, which is why the creature was given a name that means 'whale lizard'. At first, scientists thought Cetiosaurus was a sea animal, until fossils of the leg bones were found.*

R 3078

F-6

Cetiosaurus

18 metres in length

◐ *A young* Cetiosaurus *follows its parent across open ground. The adult would protect its young as well as teaching it how to survive.*

UNDER ATTACK

Some dinosaurs lived together in groups called herds. **The fully grown adults would join together to protect the youngsters.**

Herds of animals work together. If a hunter, such as *Tyrannosaurus* (tie-rann-oh-saw-rus), threatened to attack a herd of *Triceratops* (try-ser-ah-tops), they would form a circle.

The adults stood on the outside of the circle with their sharp horns facing outwards to protect the youngsters standing on the inside. *Tyrannosaurus* would be unable to reach the young, so it would give up the hunt and leave.

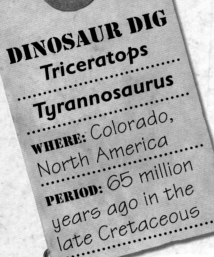

DINOSAUR DIG

Triceratops ....

Tyrannosaurus
....

WHERE: Colorado, North America ....

PERIOD: 65 million years ago in the late Cretaceous ....

DIG SITE

WOW!

Scientists have found 20 *Tyrannosaurus* skeletons — more than of any other large hunting dinosaur.

◐ *Tyrannosaurus could not break into a circle of defending* Triceratops. *However, it may return later to try to grab a youngster by surprise.*

Tyrannosaurus

12 metres in length

● *A complete fossilized skeleton of Triceratops. Its large horns may have been used to fight other dinosaurs, including hunters.*

Triceratops

9 metres in length

GOING IT ALONE

As a young dinosaur grew older, it would become stronger and begin to learn the skills it needed to survive.

Eventually a youngster would be able to look after itself. Instead of following its parent everywhere, the youngster may gradually start to drift away and begin to live on its own.

Iguanodon (ig-wan-oh-don) fed on shrubs and small trees. A young *Iguanodon* may stay with its parent for a year or two before it left to live by itself.

DINOSAUR DIG
Iguanodon

WHERE: England, Europe

WHEN: 140 million years ago in the early Cretaceous

DIG SITE

◑ *An adult Iguanodon jawbone. A youngster would have had a similar jaw and teeth as it ate the same food.*

Iguanodon

10 metres in length

◗ A young Iguanodon tries to keep up with its parent. The adult dinosaur would gradually lose interest in its young as it grew older. Eventually they would separate.

THREAT DISPLAYS

Adults may have been forced to compete with other dinosaurs of the same type.

If there was little food, survival depended on finding good feeding grounds. It is thought that some hunters may have had a home area, or territory, where they would not allow others of their kind to hunt.

DINOSAUR DIG
Dilophosaurus

WHERE: Arizona, North America

WHEN: 190 million years ago in the early Jurassic

DIG SITE

WOW!

The bones in the crests of Dilophosaurus were as thin as paper in places.

Dilophosaurus (die-low-fo-saw-rus) had a pair of bony **crests** growing from the top of its **skull**. Scientists believe that the dinosaur may have used these crests in a threat display to scare away hunters.

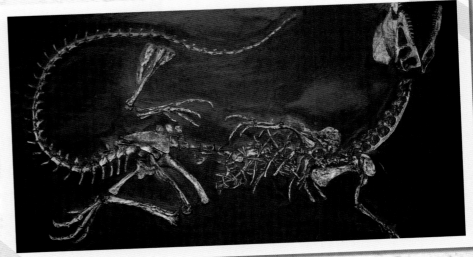

This fossil of Dilophosaurus *is almost complete, although some of the bones have become mixed up. The crests on its head can clearly be seen.*

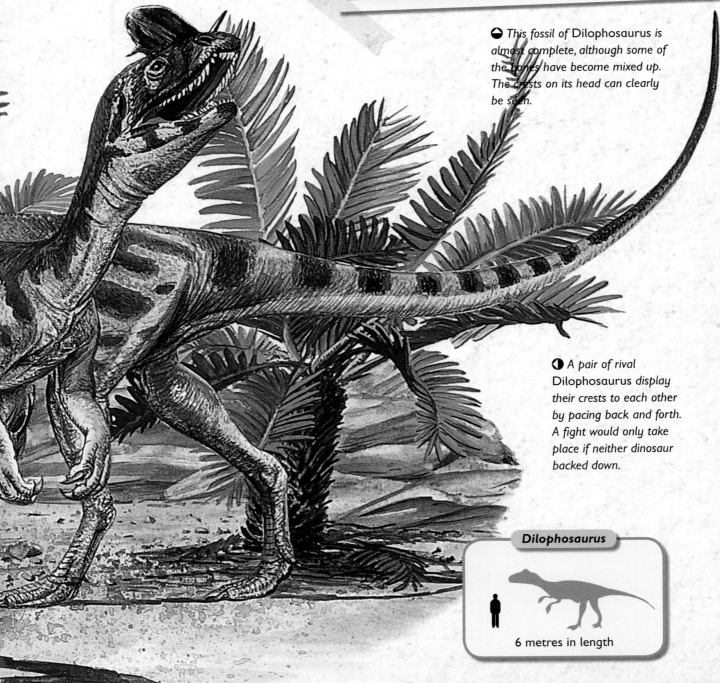

A pair of rival Dilophosaurus *display their crests to each other by pacing back and forth. A fight would only take place if neither dinosaur backed down.*

Dilophosaurus

6 metres in length

POWER STRUGGLE

Sometimes threats and displays would not settle a struggle between dinosaurs. They would often fight to decide which was the strongest.

Stegoceras (steg-oh-sair-ass) was a **bonehead** dinosaur. It had a very thick skull with a dome of solid bone on top of its head. Some scientists think that *Stegoceras* fought each other using their heads.

DINOSAUR DIG
Stegoceras

WHERE: Montana, North America

WHEN: 75 million years ago in the late Cretaceous

DIG SITE

🔘 *Stegoceras fought by charging towards each other. The force used when they crashed together would soon show which dinosaur was the strongest.*

WOW!

Stegoceras skulls could be as much as 8 centimetres in thickness. Males had thicker skulls than females.

Stegoceras would run at each other with their heads lowered. They would crash together with enormous force. After a few impacts, the weaker dinosaur would give up the fight. Scientists believe that they probably hit each other on the sides of the body, rather than head-butting.

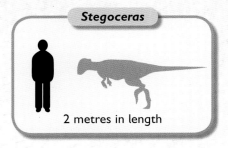

Stegoceras

2 metres in length

25

HERD INSTINCT

Some sauropods, such as *Mamenchisaurus* (ma-men-key-saw-rus), lived in herds – from as few as ten dinosaurs to as many as 100.

Living in a herd had advantages because one or two dinosaurs would always be looking out for danger. The dinosaurs could join forces to drive off a hunter. In a herd, plant eaters could find water or good eating grounds more easily.

DINOSAUR DIG
Mamenchisaurus

WHERE: China, Asia

WHEN: 150 million years ago in the late Jurassic

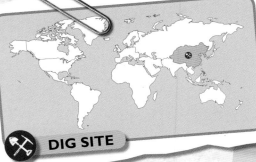

DIG SITE

◗ Mamenchisaurus *may have been able to rear up on its back legs, using the tail to balance. Then Mamenchisaurus could feed on even higher leaves on trees.*

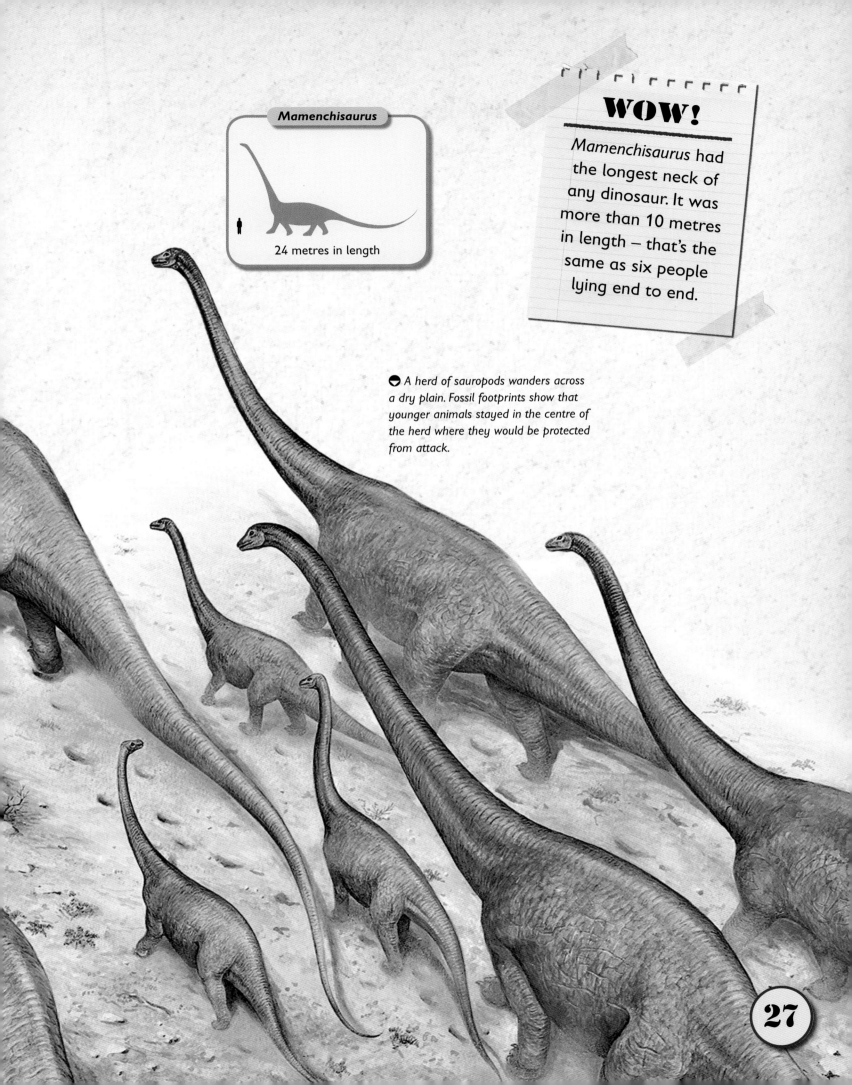

Mamenchisaurus

24 metres in length

A herd of sauropods wanders across a dry plain. Fossil footprints show that younger animals stayed in the centre of the herd where they would be protected from attack.

All dinosaurs eventually died. Some were killed by hunters or died after a fight. Others fell victim to disease or to an accident. Some probably just died of old age.

Leaellynasaura (lee-ell-in-ah-saw-rah) lived in Australia. Millions of years ago, the winters would have been very cold. If *Leaellynasaura* could not keep warm enough, it may have died from the cold.

When a dinosaur died, its body was most likely either to be eaten by the first hunter to find it or to rot away completely. The bones or teeth of only a few creatures remained as fossils.

A dinosaur that died next to a river had a better chance of being fossilized as its body would have been quickly covered by mud or sand.

DINOSAUR DIG
Leaellynasaura

WHERE: Victoria, Australia

WHEN: 110 million years ago in the mid Cretaceous

DIG SITE

WOW!

A large number of bones has been found in Alberta, Canada. Scientists believe that hundreds of dinosaurs were swept away by a fast-flowing river.

A dead Leaellynasaura lies beside a frozen river. It is thought that the long, cold winters may have killed off many weaker dinosaurs.

Leaellynasaura

2 metres in length

FOOD

Did you know that the biggest dinosaurs had the smallest mouths?

Or that some dinosaurs had super-strong jaws to clamp down on their prey?

Read on to discover everything you need to know about hunting and eating...

DINOSAUR SNAPPERS

DIG SITE

Some dinosaur hunters were fairly small. They lived by hunting animals that were smaller than themselves.

They had to be able to move quickly and easily to catch their prey. These hunters could leap and change direction suddenly.

Staurikosaurus (store-ick-oh-saw-rus) was a small hunter that ran quickly on its back legs, snapping up food in its mouth. Scientists are not certain to which dinosaur family it belonged.

Eoraptor (ee-oh-rap-tor) probably fed on small animals. It would run quickly after its prey and then tear the victim apart with its small, sharp teeth.

Staurikosaurus

2 metres in length

◖ Staurikosaurus *would eat anything that it could catch, including large insects.*

● *Eoraptor is the earliest known dinosaur. It may have used its sharp claws to dig for food or to grab smaller animals.*

Eoraptor

1 metre in length

WOW!

Eoraptor had small teeth, so it probably only hunted small animals.

◗ *A scientist cleans an Eoraptor* **skull** *to remove the surrounding stone. The process can take weeks and needs great care.*

LIZARD EATERS

Some early dinosaurs, such as *Coelophysis* (see-low-fye-sis), hunted lizards and other small animals, **including** mammals **and** amphibians.

The skeleton of *Coelophysis* was made up of slender, thin bones that were very light. This enabled *Coelophysis* to move quickly and change direction easily.

The long neck of *Coelophysis* could twist, so that the head could dart forwards to snap up prey. The front legs had clawed hands that were used for digging in soil to find food.

DINOSAUR DIG
Coelophysis

WHERE: New Mexico, North America

PERIOD: 225 million years ago in the late Triassic

DIG SITE

WOW!

A *Coelophysis* skull was taken into space to the *Mir* space station in 1998.

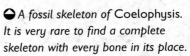 A fossil skeleton of Coelophysis. It is very rare to find a complete skeleton with every bone in its place.

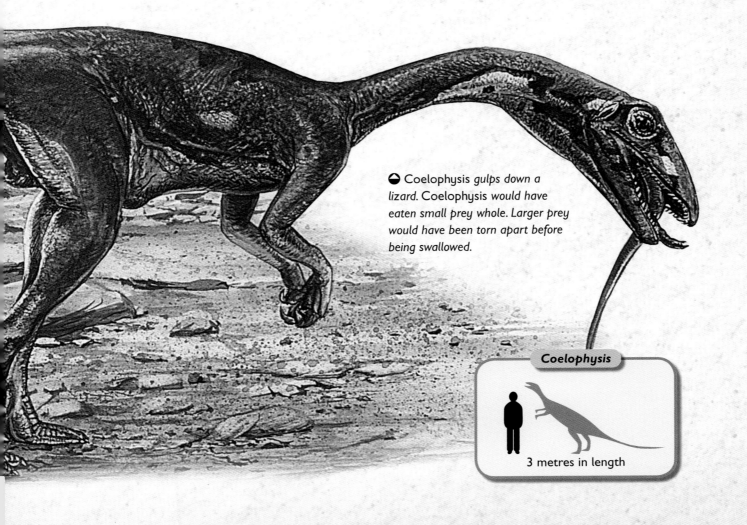

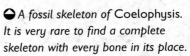 Coelophysis *gulps down a lizard.* Coelophysis *would have eaten small prey whole. Larger prey would have been torn apart before being swallowed.*

Coelophysis

3 metres in length

PLANT EATERS

Dinosaurs were a very successful group of animals. They soon took over from other types of reptile **that had ruled the Earth up until the Triassic Period.**

The first dinosaurs were all quite small, but soon larger types began to appear. *Plateosaurus* (plat-ee-oh-saw-rus) was one of the first big plant eaters, growing up to 8 metres in length with a heavy body and thick legs.

◑ Plateosaurus *had jagged, or serrated, teeth that were suited to shredding tough leaves of tree ferns and other large plants of the time.*

DINOSAUR DIG
Plateosaurus
WHERE: Germany, Europe

PERIOD: 215 million years ago in the late Triassic

⚒ **DIG SITE**

Plateosaurus

8 metres in length

Plateosaurus walked on all four legs most of the time, but could rear up on its back legs to reach leaves at the top of trees.

The front feet had a large claw on the thumb, which may have been used to dig up roots for *Plateosaurus* to eat.

⬤ *This fossilized skeleton of* Plateosaurus *has been reconstructed standing upright to show its great size.*

STRIPPING LEAVES

Sauropod dinosaurs were the biggest dinosaurs of all, but they had the smallest mouths.

The leaves and shoots that sauropods ate did not give much energy. As they were so big, sauropods needed to eat huge amounts every day to survive.

It is thought that sauropods did not chew their food at all. They bit off a mouthful of leaves and swallowed them immediately. Sauropods swallowed stones that were moved about by the stomach muscles to mash up the leaves and twigs.

DINOSAUR DIG
Brachiosaurus

WHERE: Colorado, North America

PERIOD: 150 million years ago in the late Jurassic

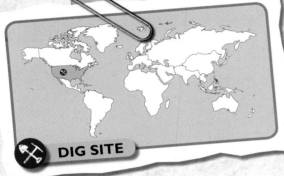

DIG SITE

◑ *A fossilized skull of Brachiosaurus (brack-ee-oh-saw-rus). The large openings in the skull are for the eyes and nostrils. The huge nostrils may have contained veins carrying blood that could be cooled by the air as it was breathed in.*

WOW!

Sauropods had such a long neck that food did not arrive in their stomach until 30 seconds after they swallowed it.

● Brachiosaurus *prepares to take a mouthful of leaves from a tree. Its long neck allowed Brachiosaurus to eat food that other dinosaurs could not reach.*

Brachiosaurus

25 metres in length

DESERT DWELLERS

The weather during the early Jurassic Period was generally warm and wet.

There may have also been very dry areas, called **deserts**, or long periods of time without rain, called droughts.

The animals that lived in these areas had to survive in dry conditions as well as in the wet. *Lufengosaurus* (loo-fung-oh-saw-rus) was a plant-eating dinosaur with sharp teeth to shred up tough plant food. The large claws on its front legs helped it to dig for food and water.

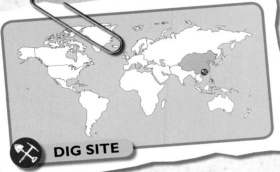

DINOSAUR DIG
Lufengosaurus

WHERE: Lufeng, China, Asia

PERIOD: 200 million years ago in the early Jurassic

DIG SITE

◑ Lufengosaurus *could eat tough fernlike plants. Its sharp teeth were ideally suited to this sort of food.*

Lufengosaurus

6 metres in length

40

The plants were digested in an enormous stomach, which was positioned in front of the back legs. The weight of its stomach meant that *Lufengosaurus* and similar dinosaurs found it easier to walk on all four legs.

◐ *The fossil skeleton of Lufengosaurus has been reconstructed to rear up. This shows how it used its neck to reach high into a tree to find food.*

WOW!

Some scientsits believe that the plant eater, *Jingshanosaurus* (yin-shahn-oh-saw-rus), may have also eaten shellfish.

WATERY WORLD

All animals need to drink water in order to survive. Water is used to help chemical processes inside the body.

Dinosaurs, like all reptiles, had skin that was covered in tough scales. These scales were waterproof and also stopped their body from losing water. Dinosaurs could then store water in their body, so they needed to drink less water than other animals.

DINOSAUR DIG
Huayangosaurus

WHERE: China, Asia

PERIOD: 165 million years ago in the mid Jurassic

DIG SITE

Huayangosaurus

4 metres in length

◗ Huayangosaurus (hoo-ah-yang-oh-saw-rus) drinks from a stream. This dinosaur lived at a time when the climate was warm and wet, so there was a ways plenty of water to drink.

◗ A fossil skeleton of Huayangosaurus shows the low position of the head. This allowed the dinosaur to feast on shrubs and other low-growing plants.

CLEVER FEEDING

Over time, dinosaurs adapted, or changed, so they could find food successfully. Some were quick, some were huge, and others had specialized body parts.

The plant-eating **ornithopod** had a long, muscular tongue to pull leaves into its mouth. The leaves were then bitten off using the sharp beak at the front of its jaws. Finally, the ornithopod chewed the food using strong teeth at the back of its jaws.

Sauropod dinosaurs were huge plant eaters with a long neck and tail. They weighed up to 80 tonnes each and ate a huge amount of plant food every day.

DINOSAUR DIG

Camptosaurus
....
Haplocanthosaurus
....
WHERE: Colorado, North America
....
PERIOD: 150 million years ago in the late Jurassic
....

DIG SITE

◉ *Sauropods, such as Haplocanthosaurus (hap-low-kan-thoe-saw-rus) used their weight to push over tall trees, so they could reach the leaves at the top.*

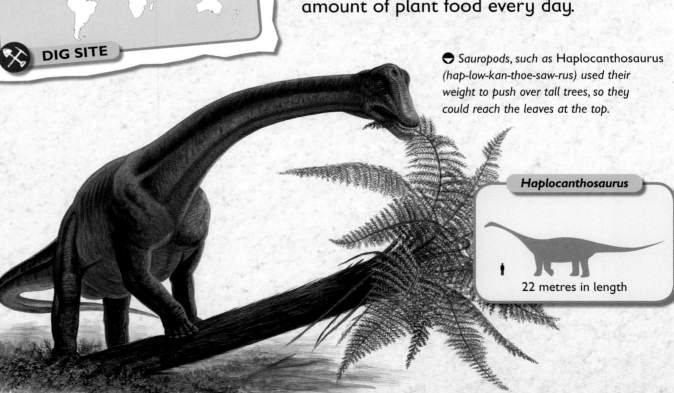

Haplocanthosaurus

22 metres in length

◖ *A fossil skeleton of* Camptosaurus *(kamp-toe-saw-rus) shows the dinosaur walking on its back legs, although it could also walk on all four.*

WOW!

For many years, scientists did not realize that *Camptosaurus* had cheeks — most reptiles do not have cheeks at all.

⬭ Camptosaurus *had a skull that was long and low compared to that of other similar dinosaurs. This allowed space for hundreds of teeth, which were used to chew up food.*

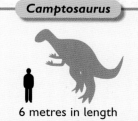

Camptosaurus

6 metres in length

THE SOUND OF FOOD

Animals rely on their sense of hearing, especially if they live in dense forests where it is difficult to see for more than a few metres.

Hunters listen out for prey, and plant eaters try to hear if a hunter is nearby. Dinosaur ears were fairly simple. It is thought that they did not have ear flaps. There was probably just a simple hole leading to the ear mechanism.

WOW!

If a dinosaur put its jaws on the ground, it could 'hear' vibrations made by the footsteps of nearby animals.

◗ Allosaurus (al-oh-saw-rus) stops to listen to a sound – it may be prey nearby. Hearing is a key sense for hunting animals and may make the difference between a successful hunt and hunger.

◐ A fossilized skeleton of Allosaurus. The large, powerful head and strong claws on the front limbs show it was an active hunter.

Allosaurus was a large hunter that probably preyed on sauropods, preferring to attack old or weak individuals as they would be easier to kill.

Allosaurus

12 metres in length

47

ON THE SCENT

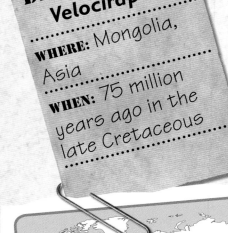

🔨 **DIG SITE**

The sense of smell is important to most animals. Plant eaters can smell a hunter from some distance away and may flee before it becomes a danger.

Hunters use scent to track down prey. Also, if the wind is blowing away from the hunter, their victim will not be able to smell them approaching.

The parts of the nose that are used to smell are never fossilized. Therefore, scientists cannot be certain how well dinosaurs could smell. However, some species have long, twisted nostrils as if they contained scent receptors, so these dinosaurs could probably smell better than others.

◗ *A **pack** of Velociraptor (vel-oss-ee-rap-tor) moves through a Cretaceous forest. There is some evidence that these dinosaurs hunted as a group, working together to find and overcome prey.*

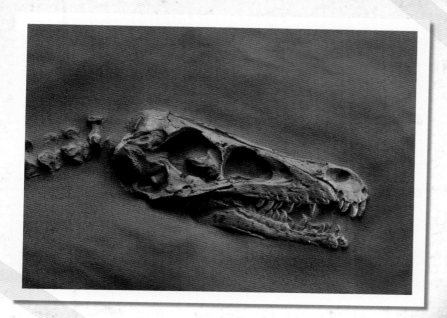

 This fossilized skull of a Velociraptor shows that this dinosaur had around 80 sharp, curved teeth set in long narrow jaws. This was ideal for eating meat once prey had been killed.

Velociraptor

2 metres in length

There were small plant eaters as well as giant sauropods. These dinosaurs may have fed in the undergrowth.

Smaller plant eaters had plenty of food because they could feed on shorter plants that larger dinosaurs missed. They could also hide from danger in the undergrowth.

DINOSAUR DIG

Micropachy-cephalosaurus

WHERE: Shandong, China, Asia

WHEN: 77 million years ago in the late Cretaceous

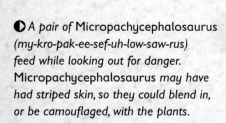

DIG SITE

◑ *A pair of Micropachycephalosaurus (my-kro-pak-ee-sef-uh-low-saw-rus) feed while looking out for danger. Micropachycephalosaurus may have had striped skin, so they could blend in, or be camouflaged, with the plants.*

Micropachycephalosaurus

0.5 metres in length

Micropachycephalosaurus lived among the undergrowth and small plants. They nibbled at leaves and shoots rather than gulping down lots of plant food.

WOW!

Micropachycephalosaurus has the longest name of any dinosaur.

TREE EATERS

Some sauropods had front legs that were much longer than their back legs. They may also have held their neck upright.

The tallest sauropod was *Sauroposeidon* (saw-roh-pos-eye-don). Its body measured 18 metres in height – as tall as two houses! These dinosaurs used their neck to feed on leaves at the top of conifer trees.

Sauroposeidon was the last sauropod with long front legs. About 95 million years ago, it became **extinct**.

DINOSAUR DIG
Sauroposeidon
....
WHERE: Oklahoma, North America
....
WHEN: 100 million years ago in the early Cretaceous
....

⚒ **DIG SITE**

Sauroposeidon

30 metres in length

⬤ *Sauroposeidon uses its great height to nibble at the top of a conifer tree. Tall trees were out of reach for smaller plant eaters.*

◉ Amargasaurus (ah-mar-gah-saw-rus) was found in Argentina, South America. It may have had flaps of skin connecting the rods of bone that grew up from its neck and back. This was probably used to scare away other dinosaurs.

WOW!

Sauroposeidon was named after the Greek god Poseidon because he was the 'Earthshaker', and the Earth probably shook when *Sauroposeidon* moved around.

Amargasaurus

10 metres in length

◑ Scientists work to put together a fossilized skeleton of Amargasaurus. Putting the bones into the correct positions is a skilled task.

53

HANDS-ON FEEDING

Some dinosaurs had front legs with special features that were used to help with feeding.

The arms of *Deinocheirus* (day-no-kye-rus) were 2.6 metres in length with hooked claws on the end that were both sharp and strong.

Some palaeontologists think that *Deinocheirus* used its claws to hook and pull down tree branches so that it could eat the leaves. Others think that it used them to dig in the ground to find roots or insects.

DINOSAUR DIG
Deinocheirus

WHERE: Mongolia, Asia

WHEN: 70 million years ago in the late Cretaceous

DIG SITE

◗ Deinocheirus *had the largest arms and claws of any dinosaur. The claws would have been even larger than shown here as they were covered in horn.*

● Some scientists believe that Deinocheirus *may have had feathers to keep it warm. Others believe that its skin was actually like that of a reptile.*

Deinocheirus

11 metres in length

POWERFUL JAWS

The very last group of dinosaurs were the ceratopians. **They had unusual teeth and jaws.**

Very powerful muscles closed the jaws, while the teeth were arranged to slice food up into tiny pieces before it was swallowed. Scientists think that ceratopians, such as *Leptoceratops* (lep-toe-ser-ah-tops), may have feasted on the leaves and twigs of flowering shrubs.

Meat eaters such as *Albertosaurus* (al-bert-oh-saw-rus) had muscles that could clamp the jaws together with great force, but the muscles that opened the jaws were much weaker.

DINOSAUR DIG

Albertosaurus ....

Leptoceratops ....

WHERE: Alberta, North America ....

WHEN: 70 million years ago in the late Cretaceous ....

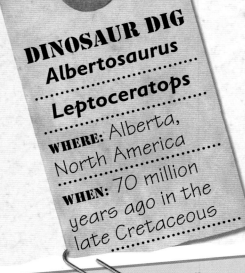

DIG SITE

⊖ Leptoceratops *fed on small plants. It bit off leaves using its beaklike mouth.*

Leptoceratops

3 metres in length

A fossil skeleton of Albertosaurus is shown with its body bent forwards. This gave the dinosaur balance when it walked.

Albertosaurus

9 metres in length

Albertosaurus *stands upright to guard its kill — a young ceratopian dinosaur.*

WOW!

In 2000, Philip Currie and his team found 12 *Albertosaurus* skeletons in Alberta, Canada. This showed that they probably lived and hunted in packs.

A TASTY SNACK

DIG SITE

It is usually thought that larger hunters preyed on large plant eaters.

However, even the biggest hunter would have snapped up a much smaller animal if it got the chance. A baby dinosaur or other small creature would have been killed instantly by one bite of the giant jaws.

Scientists think that the big hunters had such strong chemicals in their stomach that they may have been able to digest the bones. Others think that the bones were **regurgitated** from the stomach once the meat had been digested.

WOW!

Tarbosaurus lived in Asia and *Tyrannosaurus* (tie-rann-oh-saw-rus) in America, but they were very similar. Some scientists believe they were the same animal.

Tarbosaurus was a tyrannosaur that grew to be about 12 metres in length. Like other tyrannosaurs, it had very powerful jaws, but tiny front claws. Some scientists think that *Tarbosaurus* could not tackle large dinosaurs, so it fed on smaller animals or **carrion**.

● *The fossilized head and neck of* Tarbosaurus *show that this dinosaur had a deep snout and jaws attached to very powerful muscles. Its bite was probably strong enough to crush bones.*

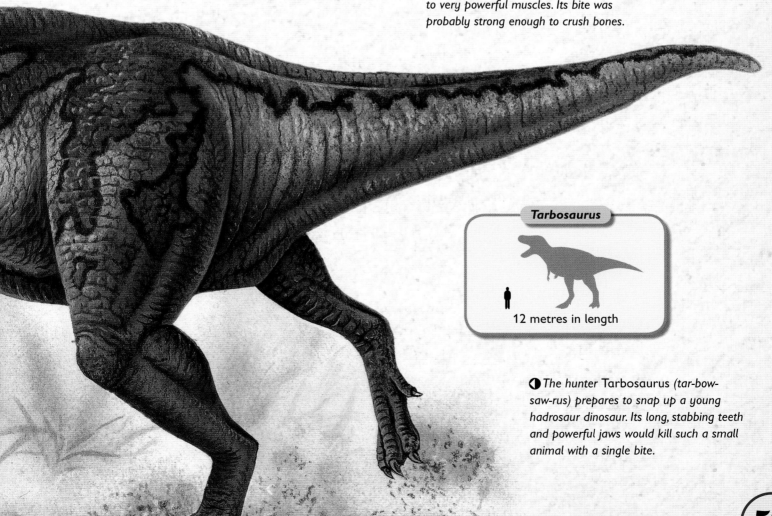

Tarbosaurus

12 metres in length

◑ *The hunter* Tarbosaurus *(tar-bow-saw-rus) prepares to snap up a young hadrosaur dinosaur. Its long, stabbing teeth and powerful jaws would kill such a small animal with a single bite.*

INTO THE FUTURE

Palaeontologists believe that birds come from small hunting dinosaurs. They both have feathers, walk on their back legs and have hollow limb bones.

Some scientists think that the two groups are so similar that they should belong to a single group. They believe that dinosaurs did not become extinct, they just became birds instead.

DINOSAUR DIG
Archaeopteryx

WHERE: Southern Germany, Europe

PERIOD: 155 million years ago in the late Jurassic

DIG SITE

Other scientists point out the differences between the groups. Dinosaurs had teeth, birds do not. Birds can fly, most dinosaurs could not. These scientists think that dinosaurs and birds should continue to be seen as different groups of animals.

WOW!

Some scientists think that birds come from a particular family of dinosaurs called the tetanurans, which later **evolved** into the tyrannosaurs.

This fossilized Archaeopteryx (ark-ee-op-tur-iks) shows the feathers and how they are arranged to form two wings. When this fossil was found, it showed a link between dinosaurs and birds.

Archaeopteryx

0.5 metres in length

Archaeopteryx perches on a tree branch. Scientists think that Archaeopteryx was a good flyer, but only over short distances.

EXPLORING THE AIR

Microraptor (my-krow-rap-tor), meaning 'tiny hunter', was named by the scientist who found it because it looked like a small hunting dinosaur.

Then it was noticed that the dinosaur had feathers growing from its arms, legs and tail. The feathers were long and strong, like those of a modern bird wing. However, its muscles were not strong enough to enable it to fly.

DINOSAUR DIG
Microraptor

WHERE: Liaoning, China, Asia

PERIOD: 130 million years ago in the early Cretaceous

DIG SITE

◑ A Microraptor *fossil preserved in rock. The feathers can be clearly seen around the bones. Delicate features, such as feathers, are rarely preserved.*

It is now thought that *Microraptor* used its feathers to glide for short distances. It may have lived in forests where it climbed trees to look for insects to feed on. The tail was probably used to control steering in the air.

⬤ *Microraptor probably glided from one tree to the next to escape from danger or to pounce on food.*

Microraptor

60 centimetres in length

WOW!

In 1999, a man glued the front end of a *Microraptor* fossil to the back end of a different dinosaur fossil. He then pretended that he had found a new type of dinosaur, but the truth was soon revealed.

HIBERNATION

Although the Earth was warmer and wetter during the time of the dinosaurs, there were areas with cooler weather.

Australia and New Zealand lay close to the South Pole about 110 million years ago. During winter, the sun did not shine for weeks on end. The weather was very cold and no plants could grow.

Some of the larger dinosaurs may have walked to warmer areas in winter, but smaller dinosaurs could not escape. Instead, they hibernated.

When an animal hibernates it goes into a very deep sleep. The heart rate and breathing slow down, the body temperature drops and all bodily functions become slower. During this time, the creature survives on fat stored in its body.

DINOSAUR DIG
Leaellynasaura
Timimus

WHERE: Southern Australia

PERIOD: 106 million years ago in the early Cretaceous

DIG SITE

WOW!

Scientists did not know that dinosaurs lived in cold parts of the world until the fossil of *Leaellynasaura* was found in Australia in the late 1900s.

◗ *A scene from Australia about 106 million years ago. The larger dinosaur* Timimus *(tim-ee-mus) hibernates under a log while a group of smaller* Leaellynasaura *(lee-ell-in-ah-saw-rah) look up at the Southern Lights.*

Leaellynasaura

2 metres in length

Timimus

3.5 metres in length

SURVIVAL

The ceratopian dinosaurs became very successful in North America because the plants on which they fed grew everywhere.

All ceratopians had beaks that they used to crop plant food and slicing teeth to cut it up before swallowing.

About 65 million years ago, dinosaurs became extinct. It is likely that the plants that plant eaters ate died out, leaving them without any food. Once the plant eaters began to disappear, meat eaters were left with no food either.

◑ Styracosaurus (sty-rak-oh-saw-rus) feeds on plants on the ground. Scientists have found thousands of Styracosaurus fossils, but only one is of a complete skull.

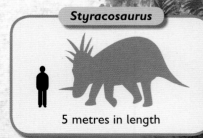

Styracosaurus

5 metres in length

◒ The patterned **neck frill** of Chasmosaurus *(kaz-mo-saw-rus)* would have been used in threat displays to scare away hunters.

Chasmosaurus

6 metres in length

◔ Chasmosaurus *had large holes in its neck frill to lighten the weight on its neck.*

COMBAT

Did you know that some dinosaurs used their neck frill to look bigger and stronger?

Or that some dinosaurs hunted in packs?

Read on to discover everything you need to know about dinosaurs in combat…

THE HUNTERS

Hunting dinosaurs had many different weapons for attacking their prey, such as teeth and claws.

Some hunters worked alone, but others lived in groups called **packs**. If a pack of small hunters attacked a larger hunter, the fight would be dramatic.

Herrerasaurus (he-ray-ra-saw-rus) was one of the largest hunters of the late Triassic Period. With sharp teeth, it was very ferocious. *Herrerasaurus* could catch smaller dinosaurs, such as *Eoraptor* (ee-oh-rap-tor), with a single bite. If *Eoraptor* formed a pack, they might stand a chance of survival.

DINOSAUR DIG

Eoraptor

Herrerasaurus

WHERE: Argentina, South America

PERIOD: 225 million years ago in the late Triassic

DIG SITE

◑ *A pack of* Eoraptor *attack a much larger* Herrerasaurus. *The larger dinosaur is more powerful, but a pack of smaller dinosaurs would be able to fight together.*

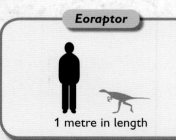

Eoraptor

1 metre in length

A fossilized **skull** of Herrerasaurus shows the curved-back teeth that helped the dinosaur to grip struggling prey.

WOW!

Fossils from the Triassic Period – the earliest time when the dinosaurs lived – show that the first dinosaurs probably lived in South America.

Herrerasaurus

3 metres in length

CARRION EATERS

Hunting dinosaurs did not always have to find and kill their prey. Sometimes they found a meal just waiting to be eaten.

A dead body, or **carcass**, that has begun to rot is called **carrion**. Some meat eaters had an extremely good sense of smell and sight to help them to find carrion. They rarely hunted at all. However, even the strongest hunters would feed on carrion if they came across it.

DINOSAUR DIG
Dromaeosaurus

WHERE: Canada, North America

PERIOD: 75 million years ago in the late Cretaceous

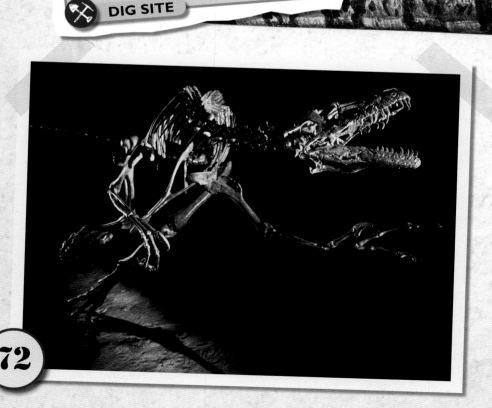

⊕ **DIG SITE**

◐ Dromaeosaurus *(drom-ee-oh-saw-rus) was equipped with excellent killing weapons — fanglike teeth and very sharp claws.*

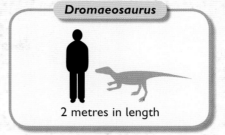

Dromaeosaurus

2 metres in length

A group of hunters squabbles over the carcass of a rhynchosaur. Although Dromaeosaurus could easily catch prey, it would also feed on carrion.

TAIL SPIKES

Plant-eating dinosaurs needed to be able to protect themselves from hunters in order to survive.

One group of dinosaurs, called **stegosaurs**, developed long, sharp spikes on their tail. *Kentrosaurus* (ken-troe-saw-rus) was a stegosaur with upright plates of bone along its back, as well as sharp spikes along its tail.

If *Kentrosaurus* faced a large hunter, such as *Allosaurus* (al-oh-saw-rus), it would easily be defeated. The only chance *Kentrosaurus* had of surviving was to hit *Allosaurus* with its tail spikes. This would injure the hunter and *Kentrosaurus* could escape.

DINOSAUR DIG

Allosaurus

Kentrosaurus

WHERE: Tanzania, Africa

PERIOD: 150 million years ago in the late Jurassic

DIG SITE

WOW!

The bone spikes of *Kentrosaurus* would have been covered in shiny horn with extremely sharp points, making them excellent weapons.

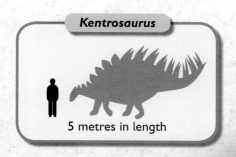

Kentrosaurus

5 metres in length

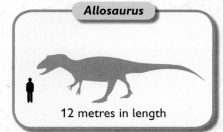

A fossil skeleton of Allosaurus shows how it might stride forwards while hunting. The head could lunge out to bite prey.

Allosaurus

12 metres in length

Allosaurus *attacks* Kentrosaurus. *The hunter is more than twice as large, so Kentrosaurus had to use all its power to escape from Allosaurus.*

DINOSAUR RUNNERS

Dinosaurs could run well. This skill was important for chasing prey and escaping from danger.

As dinosaur legs grew straight down from the hips, they only needed to move their legs in order to walk or run. Other reptiles need to swing their body from side to side because their legs grow out from the sides. Therefore, dinosaurs could move faster while using less energy than many other reptiles.

Coelophysis (see-low-fye-sis) was an early hunting dinosaur. It ran on its back legs. *Coelophysis* was fast and agile enough to snap up other smaller animals of the time. It was also able to flee quickly from danger.

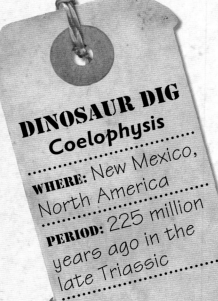

DINOSAUR DIG

Coelophysis

WHERE: New Mexico, North America

PERIOD: 225 million years ago in the late Triassic

DIG SITE

WOW!

There are two dinosaur groups. The ornithischians had hips like modern birds, and the saurischians had hips like modern lizards.

◑ *Dinosaurs and other animals flee as fire sweeps across the Triassic landscape of North America. Events such as this have been recorded in the fossil record – a list of all the fossils ever discovered.*

A **fossil** skeleton of Coelophysis. The remains of its last meal have been preserved inside its stomach.

Coelophysis

3 metres in length

THE CHASE

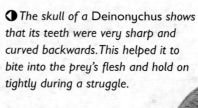

DIG SITE

Some smaller plant eaters relied on speed to escape from danger.

They had no weapons and were fairly weak, so they would run away as soon as they saw a hunter. However, many meat eaters were also able to run very quickly, so they would chase the smaller dinosaur.

If a plant eater, such as *Hypsilophodon* (hip-see-loff-oh-don), could run faster than a hunter, such as *Deinonychus* (die-non-ee-kuss), it would escape. If it could not, then it would fall victim and end up as a meal for the hunter.

◑ *The skull of a Deinonychus shows that its teeth were very sharp and curved backwards. This helped it to bite into the prey's flesh and hold on tightly during a struggle.*

78

If Deinonychus attacked a herd of Hypsilophodon, they would panic and spread out. One of them would be slower than the rest and would easily be injured by the sharp claws of Deinonychus.

Hypsilophodon

2.5 metres in length

Deinonychus

3 metres in length

79

HUNTING ALONE

A hunter working alone would have avoided attacking a large plant eater.

It would have been difficult for meat eaters, such as *Ceratosaurus* (se-rat-oh-saw-rus), to attack *Brachiosaurus* (brack-ee-oh-saw-rus) because it was so large. Although *Brachiosaurus* had no weapons, such as sharp teeth or claws, it could stamp or kick with great force. *Ceratosaurus* would need to take *Brachiosaurus* by surprise, or be very lucky, to win the combat.

DINOSAUR DIG
Brachiosaurus

Ceratosaurus

WHERE: Wyoming, North America

PERIOD: 150 million years ago in the late Jurassic

DIG SITE

◗ *This famous skeleton of a Brachiosaurus from a museum in Berlin is the largest mounted dinosaur skeleton in the world. The fossilized skeleton had several bones missing, which were replaced with fossil bones taken from other similar dinosaurs.*

Brachiosaurus

25 metres in length

● Ceratosaurus *prepares to attack an* **adult** Brachiosaurus. *Hunters would probably have preferred to avoid such large individuals and would attack younger animals instead.*

Ceratosaurus

6 metres in length

81

EASY PREY

DINOSAUR DIG
Megalosaurus
WHERE: France, Europe
PERIOD: 165 million years ago in the mid Jurassic

DIG SITE

WOW!

Fossilized sauropod bones have been found covered in scratch and bite marks – probably from the teeth of hunting dinosaurs!

Most hunters preferred to find an easier meal than fighting a fully grown sauropod. Young sauropods were easier to kill.

Young dinosaurs were smaller and weaker than adults, and they had less experience of how to fight or escape from danger.

Megalosaurus (meg-ah-low-saw-rus) was armed with sharp teeth in strong jaws, and had powerful claws on its feet. If it could catch a dinosaur smaller than itself, it would have an easy meal. Old or sick animals were also easier to overcome than healthy adults.

◑ Megalosaurus *prepares to eat a young sauropod that it has killed. It was the most powerful hunter in Europe during the late Jurassic Period.*

The teeth of Megalosaurus were very sharp and curved backwards. This would give the dinosaur a firm grip on struggling prey.

Megalosaurus

9 metres in length

FATAL WOUNDS

DINOSAUR DIG

Deinonychus ....

Tenontosaurus ....

WHERE: Oklahoma, North America ....

WHEN: 100 million years ago in the early Cretaceous ....

DIG SITE

Deinonychus (die-non-ee-kuss) **belonged to a group of ferocious hunters known as** raptors.

These fast-moving hunters had a large, curved claw on each of their back legs. This weapon was held off the ground so that it stayed sharp and ready for action.

◖ *A pack of* Deinonychus *attack* Tenontosaurus. *Scientists have found a fossil showing that* Tenontosaurus *had once been killed by a group of these hunters.*

◖ *This skeleton shows Deinonychus leaping forwards as though it were about to attack a victim.*

A group of *Deinonychus* may have pounced on a larger dinosaur and used their back claws to cause deep wounds. Then they would run off before *Tenontosaurus* (ten-on-toe-saw-rus) could fight back. They would probably wait for their prey to bleed to death, then move in to feast on the body.

Tenontosaurus

7 metres in length

Deinonychus

3 metres in length

A GAME OF BLUFF

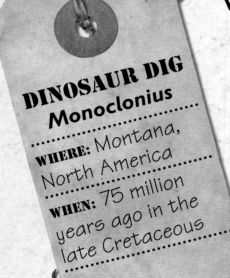

DIG SITE

When they meet a dangerous hunter or rival, many animals will try to make themselves look bigger and stronger than they really are. They hope that this will frighten off the other animal.

Many scientists think that **ceratopian** dinosaurs used their **neck frill** as a **bluffing** weapon. The frill looked large and impressive. The animal would lift up its frill so that it looked as big as possible, then move it from side to side. It was actually made of a thin layer of bone and skin. The frill may also have been used to attract females before mating.

A rare complete skeleton of Monoclonius (mon-oh-clone-ee-us). Usually only part of the skeleton is found. A skeleton such as this allows scientists to see how the complete animal appeared.

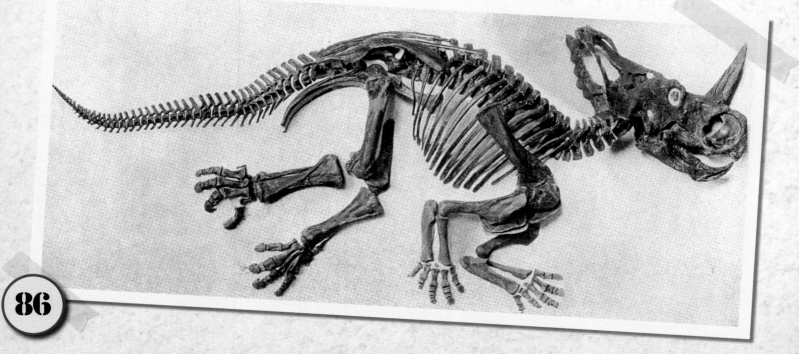

Monoclonius

5 metres in length

WOW!

The dinosaur *Centrosaurus* (sen-tro-saw-rus) was identical to *Monoclonius*, except that its horn curved forwards slightly instead of backwards.

● *Monoclonius lowers its head and stamps on the ground with its front feet as it prepares for a fight. Combats may have been between rivals of the same species, or against hunters.*

87

THE AMBUSH

DIG SITE

Tarbosaurus (tar-bow-saw-rus) was a large, powerful hunter. It had long, sharp teeth set in jaws that were powered by very strong muscles.

However, it was unable to run very quickly. The best chance it had of killing prey was to ambush it. *Tarbosaurus* would wait in bushes or behind trees, then leap out on a victim.

Scientists know a lot about *Tarbosaurus* because they have found many fossilized skeletons. Few other dinosaurs from Asia have been found in such numbers, so there must have been many of them around in the late Cretaceous Period.

◐ *The teeth of Tarbosaurus were smaller than those of its close relative Tyrannosaurus (tie-rann-oh-saw-rus).*

WOW!

The tiny arms of *Tarbosaurus* were too small to reach its mouth, so scientists are not sure what they were for.

The mouth of Tarbosaurus could be opened very wide to reveal its fangs. The wide **gape** and strong jaws show that it may have killed prey by running at them with its mouth open.

Tarbosaurus

12 metres in length

ALARM!

Plant eaters that live in herds or flocks usually have a way of warning others if danger threatens.

Some animals will call loudly or stamp their feet on the ground to make a noise. Others have brightly coloured parts of their body that they will reveal suddenly, flashing a patch of colour on and off.

DINOSAUR DIG

Anserimimus
Oviraptor
Protoceratops
Tarbosaurus

WHERE: Mongolia, Asia

WHEN: 75 million years ago in the late Cretaceous

DIG SITE

Protoceratops

2 metres in length

🔹 *A pair of* Protoceratops *(pro-toe-ser-ah-tops) guard their nest.*

Oviraptor

2 metres in length

Some dinosaurs had brightly coloured feathers growing from their tail. These may have been used as an alarm signal. The dinosaur would show the back of the fan as it fled from danger. Other dinosaurs would follow because they knew that they would also be running away from the hunting dinosaur.

● *A tyrannosaur chases* Anserimimus *(ann-sair-ee-me-mus) and* Oviraptor *(oh-vee-rap-tor).*

Anserimimus

3 metres in length

Tarbosaurus

12 metres in length

WEAPONS

When a hunter attacked prey, it would try to avoid any weapons that the plant eater had. The plant eater would do its best to use those weapons to defend itself.

Triceratops (try-ser-ah-tops) had three long, sharp horns on its head to defend itself against hunters. When *Tyrannosaurus* (tie-rann-oh-saw-rus) attacked, *Triceratops* would stab the hunter. If *Tyrannosaurus* became injured, then *Triceratops* would be able to escape.

DIG SITE

◑ *A skeleton of Tyrannosaurus shows how it would lunge forwards to attack its prey.*

Tyrannosaurus

12 metres in length

If *Tyrannosaurus* could only make one good bite, it may have stood back to wait for the plant eater to become weak through loss of blood. Then it would move in to make the kill.

● *Tyrannosaurus* battles with *Triceratops* by trying to bite into the soft sides of the plant eater while avoiding its sharp horns.

Triceratops

9 metres in length

THE TAIL CLUB

The armoured dinosaurs, or ankylosaurs, **had a unique way of defending themselves from attack.**

The back, sides, head and tail of *Pinacosaurus* (pin-ah-coe-saw-rus) had a thick armour of bone covered in horn. *Pinacosaurus* also had a heavy, bone tail club, which it would use to stop an attacker, such as *Tarbosaurus* (tar-bow-saw-rus), from flipping it over. A blow from the club could seriously injure a hunter.

DINOSAUR DIG

Pinacosaurus
....
Tarbosaurus
....
WHERE: Mongolia, Asia
....
WHEN: 80 million years ago in the late Cretaceous
....

DIG SITE

Pinacosaurus

5.5 metres in length

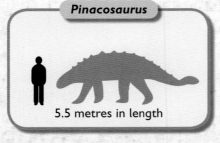

◐ The fossilized skeleton of an ankylosaur. Many skeletons are found with the bones scattered, so they need to be put back in position to show what the dinosaur looked like.

WOW!

Ankylosaurs have been found all over the world, except in Africa.

● Tarbosaurus is knocked over by a hit from the tail of Pinacosaurus. To make a successful attack, Tarbosaurus had to turn the armoured dinosaur over and attack its soft belly.

Tarbosaurus

12 metres in length

HEAD TO HEAD

If a hunting dinosaur was extremely hungry, it may risk an attack on a plant eater that was ready to defend itself.

Tyrannosaurus (tie-rann-oh-saw-rus) was a powerful killer and may sometimes have become desperate enough to attack an equally strong victim.

Styracosaurus (sty-rak-oh-saw-rus) had a huge, sharp horn growing from its nose, which could cause a serious wound to *Tyrannosaurus*.

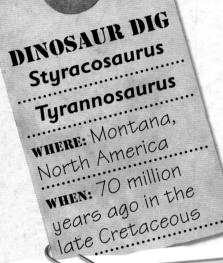

DINOSAUR DIG

Styracosaurus
....
Tyrannosaurus
....
WHERE: Montana, North America
....
WHEN: 70 million years ago in the late Cretaceous

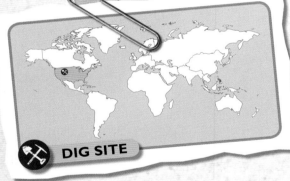

DIG SITE

WOW!

One fossil of *Styracosaurus* was found covered in charcoal. This showed that it had probably died in a forest fire.

Styracosaurus

5 metres in length

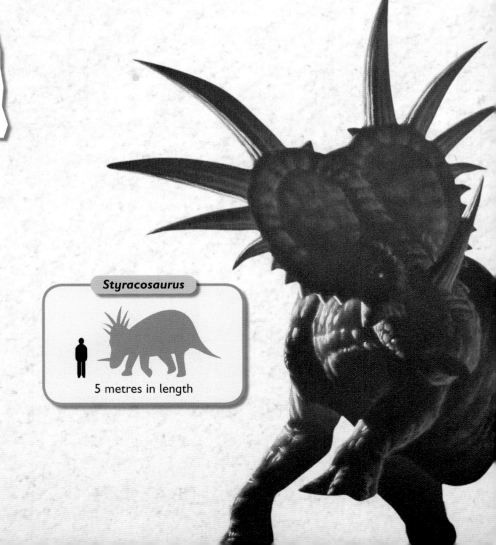

◐ *The teeth of Tyrannosaurus were only lightly fixed to the jaw and often broke off, so Tyrannosaurus constantly grew new teeth.*

⬤ Tyrannosaurus *prepares to attack* Styracosaurus. Styracosaurus *had horns on its head that pointed backwards to protect its neck and back.*

Tyrannosaurus

12 metres in length

97

FINAL BATTLE

As conditions changed, new types of dinosaur gradually evolved and older types died out.

Sauropods became much rarer and stegosaurs died out completely. They were replaced by ceratopians and hadrosaurs.

Suddenly, about 65 million years ago, all the dinosaurs became extinct. Many other types of animal died out at the same time.

Scientists are not certain what caused this mass extinction. Some think that a meteorite hit the Earth, wiping out huge numbers of animals. Others think that a sudden change in climate caused the deaths.

DINOSAUR DIG
Triceratops
Tyrannosaurus

WHERE: Colorado, North America

WHEN: 65 million years ago in the late Cretaceous

DIG SITE

This skeleton of Triceratops (try-ser-ah-tops) shows both the long, sharp horns and the large neck frill. It was a sturdy, powerful animal.

◗ Triceratops *prepares to face* Tyrannosaurus *(tie-rann-oh-saw-rus) in battle.* Tyrannosaurus *would have tried to avoid the sharp horns of its prey.*

Triceratops

9 metres in length

Tyrannosaurus

12 metres in length

DINO GUIDE

For every dinosaur in this book and many more, learn how to pronounce their name, find out their length and weight, and discover what they ate.

Coelophysis

PRONUNCIATION
see-low-fye-sis
LENGTH 3 metres
WEIGHT 35 kilograms
DIET Small animals

Efraasia

PRONUNCIATION
ef-rah-see-ah
LENGTH 7 metres
WEIGHT 600 kilograms
DIET Plants

Eoraptor

PRONUNCIATION
ee-oh-rap-tor
LENGTH 1 metre
WEIGHT 3–15 kilograms
DIET Small animals

Herrerasaurus

PRONUNCIATION
he-ray-ra-saw-rus
LENGTH 3 metres
WEIGHT 200 kilograms
DIET Animals

Melanorosaurus

PRONUNCIATION
mel-an-or-oh-saw-rus
LENGTH 10 metres
WEIGHT 1 tonne
DIET Plants

Mussaurus

PRONUNCIATION
muss-saw-rus
LENGTH 4 metres
WEIGHT 150 kilograms
DIET Plants

Pisanosaurus

PRONUNCIATION
peez-an-oh-saw-rus

LENGTH 1 metre

WEIGHT 3 kilograms

DIET Plants

Plateosaurus

PRONUNCIATION
plat-ee-oh-saw-rus

LENGTH 8 metres

WEIGHT 1 tonne

DIET Plants

Procompsognathus

PRONUNCIATION
pro-comp-sog-nay-thus

LENGTH 1.3 metres

WEIGHT 2–3 kilograms

DIET Small animals

Riojasaurus

PRONUNCIATION
ree-oh-ha-saw-rus

LENGTH 10 metres

WEIGHT 1 tonne

DIET Plants

Saltopus

PRONUNCIATION
sall-toe-puss

LENGTH Less than 1 metre

WEIGHT 1–2 kilograms

DIET Small animals

Staurikosaurus

PRONUNCIATION
store-ick-oh-saw-rus

LENGTH 2 metres

WEIGHT 30 kilograms

DIET Small animals

Allosaurus
PRONUNCIATION
al-oh-saw-rus
LENGTH 12 metres
WEIGHT 1.5–2 tonnes
DIET Animals

Anchisaurus
PRONUNCIATION
an-kee-saw-rus
LENGTH 2.5 metres
WEIGHT 35 kilograms
DIET Plants

Apatosaurus
PRONUNCIATION
ap-at-oh-saw-rus
LENGTH 25 metres
WEIGHT 25–35 tonnes
DIET Plants

Archaeopteryx
PRONUNCIATION
ark-ee-op-tur-iks
LENGTH 0.5 metres
WEIGHT 0.5 kilograms
DIET Insects and small animals

Brachiosaurus
PRONUNCIATION
brack-ee-oh-saw-rus
LENGTH 25 metres
WEIGHT 50 tonnes
DIET Plants

Camptosaurus
PRONUNCIATION
kamp-toe-saw-rus
LENGTH 6 metres
WEIGHT 1–2 tonnes
DIET Plants

Ceratosaurus
PRONUNCIATION
se-rat-oh-saw-rus
LENGTH 6 metres
WEIGHT 700–850 kilograms
DIET Animals

Cetiosaurus

PRONUNCIATION
set-ee-oh-saw-rus
LENGTH 18 metres
WEIGHT 15–20 tonnes
DIET Plants

Coelurus

PRONUNCIATION
seel-yur-rus
LENGTH 2 metres
WEIGHT 15 kilograms
DIET Animals

Compsognathus

PRONUNCIATION
comp-sog-nay-thus
LENGTH 1–1.5 metres
WEIGHT 3 kilograms
DIET Small animals

Dicraeosaurus

PRONUNCIATION
die-kree-oh-saw-rus
LENGTH 13–20 metres
WEIGHT 10 tonnes
DIET Plants

Dilophosaurus

PRONUNCIATION
die-low-fo-saw-rus
LENGTH 6 metres
WEIGHT 400 kilograms
DIET Animals

Euhelopus

PRONUNCIATION
you-hel-oh-puss
LENGTH 10–15 metres
WEIGHT 10–25 tonnes
DIET Plants

Haplocanthosaurus

PRONUNCIATION
hap-low-kan-thoe-saw-rus
LENGTH 22 metres
WEIGHT 20 tonnes
DIET Plants

Huayangosaurus
PRONUNCIATION
hoo-ah-yang-oh-saw-rus
LENGTH 4 metres
WEIGHT 400–600 kilograms
DIET Plants

Jingshanosaurus
PRONUNCIATION
yin-shahn-oh-saw-rus
LENGTH 7.5 metres
WEIGHT 1 tonne
DIET Plants

Kentrosaurus
PRONUNCIATION
ken-troe-saw-rus
LENGTH 5 metres
WEIGHT 2 tonnes
DIET Plants

Lesothosaurus
PRONUNCIATION
le-so-toe-saw-rus
LENGTH 1 metre
WEIGHT 2–3 kilograms
DIET Plants

Lufengosaurus
PRONUNCIATION
loo-fung-oh-saw-rus
LENGTH 6 metres
WEIGHT 220 kilograms
DIET Plants

Mamenchisaurus
PRONUNCIATION
ma-men-key-saw-rus
LENGTH 24 metres
WEIGHT 12–15 tonnes
DIET Plants

JURASSIC PERIOD
206 TO 145 MILLION YEARS AGO

Megalosaurus
PRONUNCIATION
meg-ah-low-saw-rus
LENGTH 9 metres
WEIGHT 1 tonne
DIET Plants

Ornitholestes
PRONUNCIATION
or-nith-oh-less-teez
LENGTH 2 metres
WEIGHT 30 kilograms
DIET Animals

Sinosauropteryx
PRONUNCIATION
sy-no-saw-op-tur-iks
LENGTH 1 metre
WEIGHT 3 kilograms
DIET Small animals

Stegosaurus
PRONUNCIATION
steg-oh-saw-rus
LENGTH 8–9 metres
WEIGHT 2–3 tonnes
DIET Plants

Supersaurus
PRONUNCIATION
soo-per-saw-rus
LENGTH 30–40 metres
WEIGHT 30–50 tonnes
DIET Plants

CRETACEOUS PERIOD
145 TO 65 MILLION YEARS AGO

Albertosaurus
PRONUNCIATION
al-bert-oh-saw-rus
LENGTH 9 metres
WEIGHT 2.5 tonnes
DIET Animals

Amargasaurus
PRONUNCIATION
ah-mar-gah-saw-rus
LENGTH 10 metres
WEIGHT 5–7 tonnes
DIET Plants

Anserimimus
PRONUNCIATION
ann-sair-ee-me-mus
LENGTH 3 metres
WEIGHT 300 kilograms
DIET Small animals

Centrosaurus
PRONUNCIATION
sen-tro-saw-rus
LENGTH 6 metres
WEIGHT 3 tonnes
DIET Plants

Chasmosaurus
PRONUNCIATION
kaz-mo-saw-rus
LENGTH 6 metres
WEIGHT 2–3 tonnes
DIET Plants

Deinonychus
PRONUNCIATION
die-non-ee-kuss
LENGTH 3 metres
WEIGHT 60 kilograms
DIET Small animals

Deinocheirus
PRONUNCIATION
day-no-kye-rus
LENGTH 11 metres
WEIGHT 4–7 tonnes
DIET Animals and plants

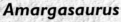

CRETACEOUS PERIOD
145 TO 65 MILLION YEARS AGO

Dromaeosaurus
PRONUNCIATION
drom-ee-oh-saw-rus
LENGTH 2 metres
WEIGHT 25 kilograms
DIET Small and medium-sized animals

Euoplocephalus
PRONUNCIATION
you-oh-ploe-sef-ah-lus
LENGTH 6–7 metres
WEIGHT 2 tonnes
DIET Plants

Hypsilophodon
PRONUNCIATION
hip-see-loff-oh-don
LENGTH 2.5 metres
WEIGHT 20–40 kilograms
DIET Plants

Iguanodon
PRONUNCIATION
ig-wan-oh-don
LENGTH 10 metres
WEIGHT 4–5 tonnes
DIET Plants

Jobaria
PRONUNCIATION
joe-barr-ee-ah
LENGTH 20 metres
WEIGHT 18–20 tonnes
DIET Plants

Leaellynasaura
PRONUNCIATION
lee-ell-in-ah-saw-rah
LENGTH 2 metres
WEIGHT 10 kilograms
DIET Plants

Leptoceratops
PRONUNCIATION
lep-toe-ser-ah-tops
LENGTH 3 metres
WEIGHT 50–200 kilograms
DIET Plants

Maiasaura
PRONUNCIATION
my-yah-saw-rah
LENGTH 9 metres
WEIGHT 3–4 tonnes
DIET Plants

Micropachycephalosaurus
PRONUNCIATION
my-kro-pak-ee-sef-uh-low-saw-rus
LENGTH 0.5 metres
WEIGHT 20 kilograms
DIET Plants

Microraptor
PRONUNCIATION
my-krow-rap-tor
LENGTH 60 centimetres
WEIGHT 1 kilogram
DIET Small animals

Monoclonius
PRONUNCIATION
mon-oh-clone-ee-us
LENGTH 5 metres
WEIGHT 2–3 tonnes
DIET Plants

Oviraptor
PRONUNCIATION
oh-vee-rap-tor
LENGTH 2 metres
WEIGHT 30 kilograms
DIET Small animals and plants

Pinacosaurus

PRONUNCIATION
pin-ah-coe-saw-rus
LENGTH 5.5 metres
WEIGHT 1–2 tonnes
DIET Plants

Protoceratops

PRONUNCIATION
pro-toe-ser-ah-tops
LENGTH 2 metres
WEIGHT 150–250 kilograms
DIET Plants

Sauroposeidon

PRONUNCIATION
saw-roh-pos-eye-don
LENGTH 30 metres
WEIGHT 50–80 tonnes
DIET Plants

Stegoceras

PRONUNCIATION
steg-oh-sair-ass
LENGTH 2 metres
WEIGHT 50–70 kilograms
DIET Plants

Stygimoloch

PRONUNCIATION
stij-ee-mol-ock
LENGTH 2–3 metres
WEIGHT 70–200 kilograms
DIET Plants

Styracosaurus

PRONUNCIATION
sty-rak-oh-saw-rus
LENGTH 5 metres
WEIGHT 3 tonnes
DIET Plants

Tarbosaurus
PRONUNCIATION
tar-bow-saw-rus
LENGTH 12 metres
WEIGHT 4 tonnes
DIET Large animals

Tenontosaurus
PRONUNCIATION
ten-on-toe-saw-rus
LENGTH 7 metres
WEIGHT 1 tonne
DIET Plants

Timimus
PRONUNCIATION
tim-ee-mus
LENGTH 3.5 metres
WEIGHT 300 kilograms
DIET Unknown

Triceratops
PRONUNCIATION
try-ser-ah-tops
LENGTH 9 metres
WEIGHT 5–8 tonnes
DIET Plants

Tyrannosaurus
PRONUNCIATION
tie-rann-oh-saw-rus
LENGTH 12 metres
WEIGHT 6 tonnes
DIET Large animals

Velociraptor
PRONUNCIATION
vel-oss-ee-rap-tor
LENGTH 2 metres
WEIGHT 20–30 kilograms
DIET Small animals

GLOSSARY

Adult
An animal that is fully grown.

Amphibian
An animal that lays its eggs in water, but lives most of its life on land.

Ankylosaur
A type of dinosaur that had armour across its back and other parts of its body.

Bluff
To deceive someone by pretending to be someone else.

Bonehead
A type of dinosaur that had a thick layer of bone on top of its skull.

Carcass
The body of a dead animal.

Carrion
Meat from a dead animal that the hunter has not killed itself.

Ceratopian
A group of dinosaurs that had a neck frill and teeth designed for slicing. Most ceratopians also had horns on their head.

Crest
Bone on the top of the head.

Cretaceous
The third period of time in the age of the dinosaurs. The Cretaceous began about 145 million years ago and ended about 65 million years ago.

Desert
A very dry area of land where few, if any, plants or animals live.

Dinosaur
A type of reptile that lived millions of years ago. All dinosaurs are now extinct.

Erode
To wear away.

Evolve
To develop gradually over a long period of time.

Extinct
Not existing any more. An animal is extinct when they have all died out.

Fossil
Any part of a plant or animal that has been preserved in rock. Also traces of plants or animals, such as footprints.

Gape
A widely opened mouth.

Hatch
To emerge from an egg.

Herd
A group of animals that lives together.

Jurassic
The second period of time in the age of the dinosaurs. The Jurassic began about 206 million years ago and ended about 145 million years ago.

Mammal
An animal that has hair or fur and produces milk for its babies.

Neck frill
A thin plate of bone and skin growing from the back of an animal's skull.

Nursery
A place where dinosaurs went to hatch their babies and where the young lived for some time afterwards.

Ornithopod
A group of plant-eating dinosaurs that had a beak and strong chewing teeth.

Pack
A group of hunting animals.

Palaeontologist
A scientist who studies ancient forms of life, including dinosaurs.

Raptor
A type of dinosaur that had a very large claw on each of its back legs.

Regurgitate
To bring swallowed food up from the stomach into the mouth.

Reptile
A cold-blooded animal, such as a lizard. Dinosaurs were reptiles, too.

Sauropod
A type of dinosaur that had a long neck and tail. Sauropods included the largest of all dinosaurs.

Skeleton
The bones in an animal's body.

Skull
The bones of the head of an animal. The skull does not include the jaw, but many skulls have jaws attached.

Stegosaur
A type of dinosaur that had upright plates or spikes growing from its back.

Triassic
The first period of time in the age of the dinosaurs. The Triassic began about 248 million years ago and ended about 208 million years ago.

Undergrowth
Bushes, small trees and other plants that grow under bigger plants and trees.

INDEX

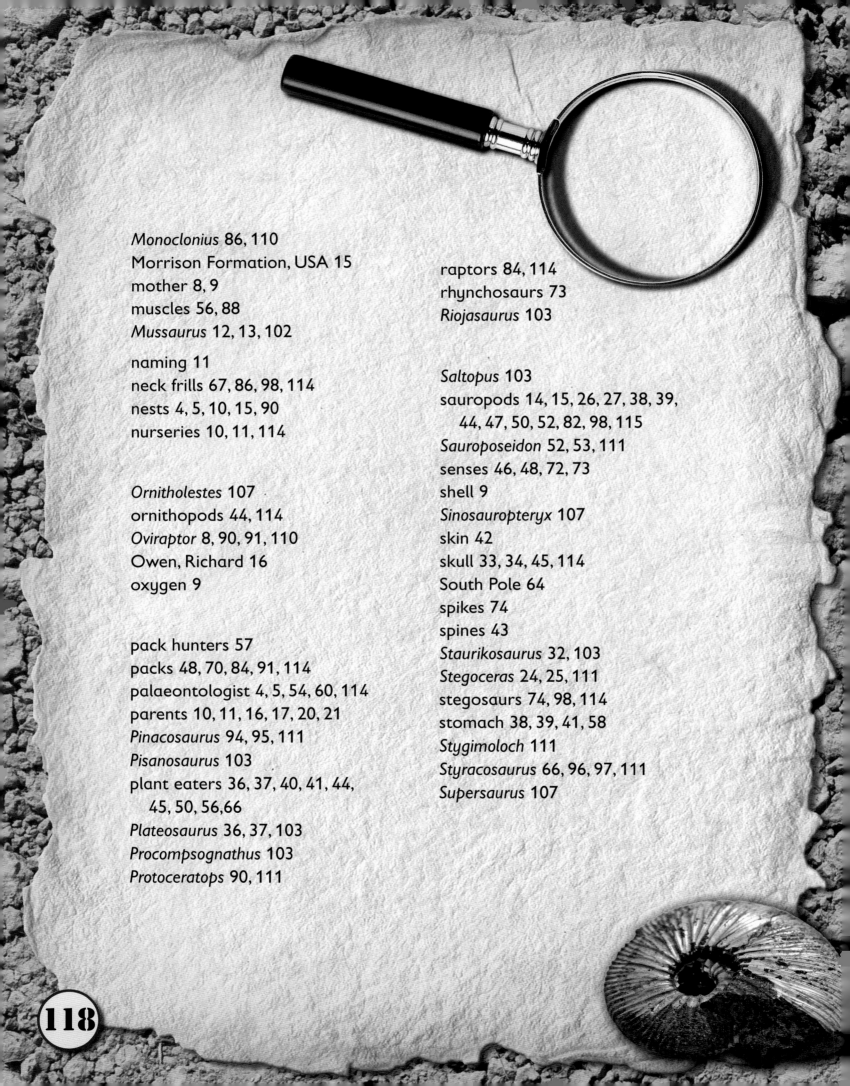

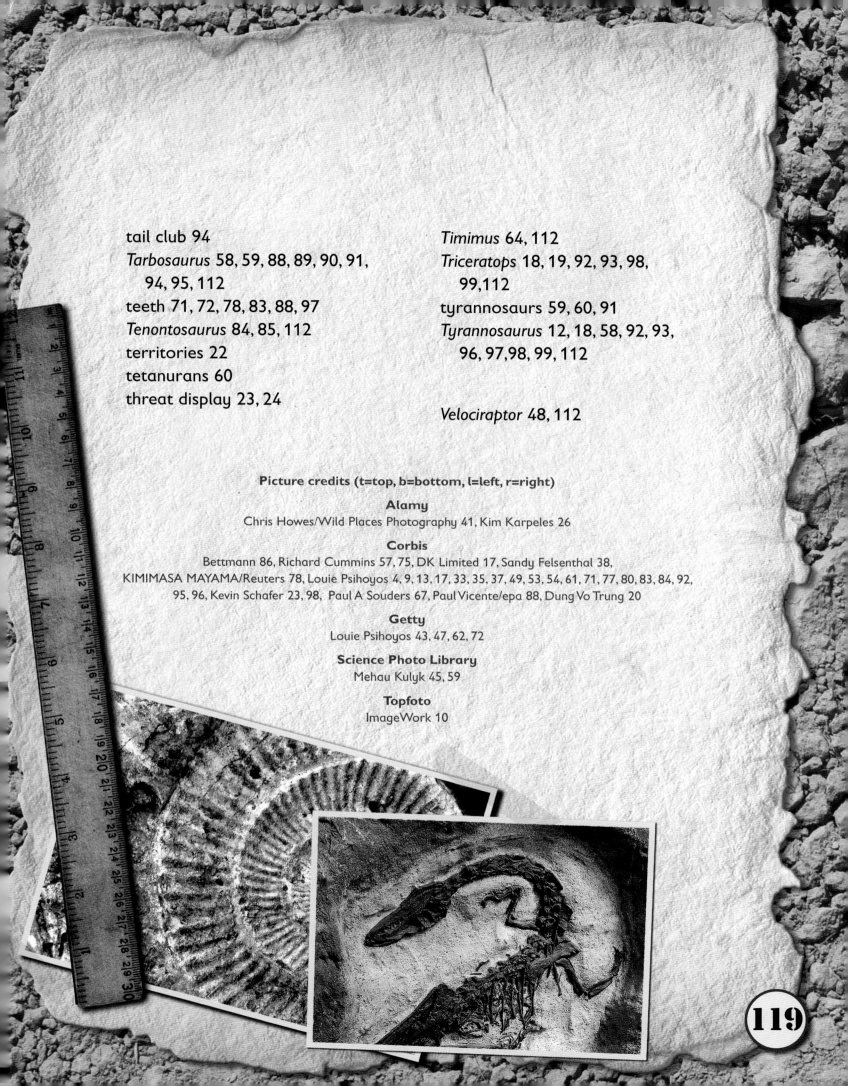

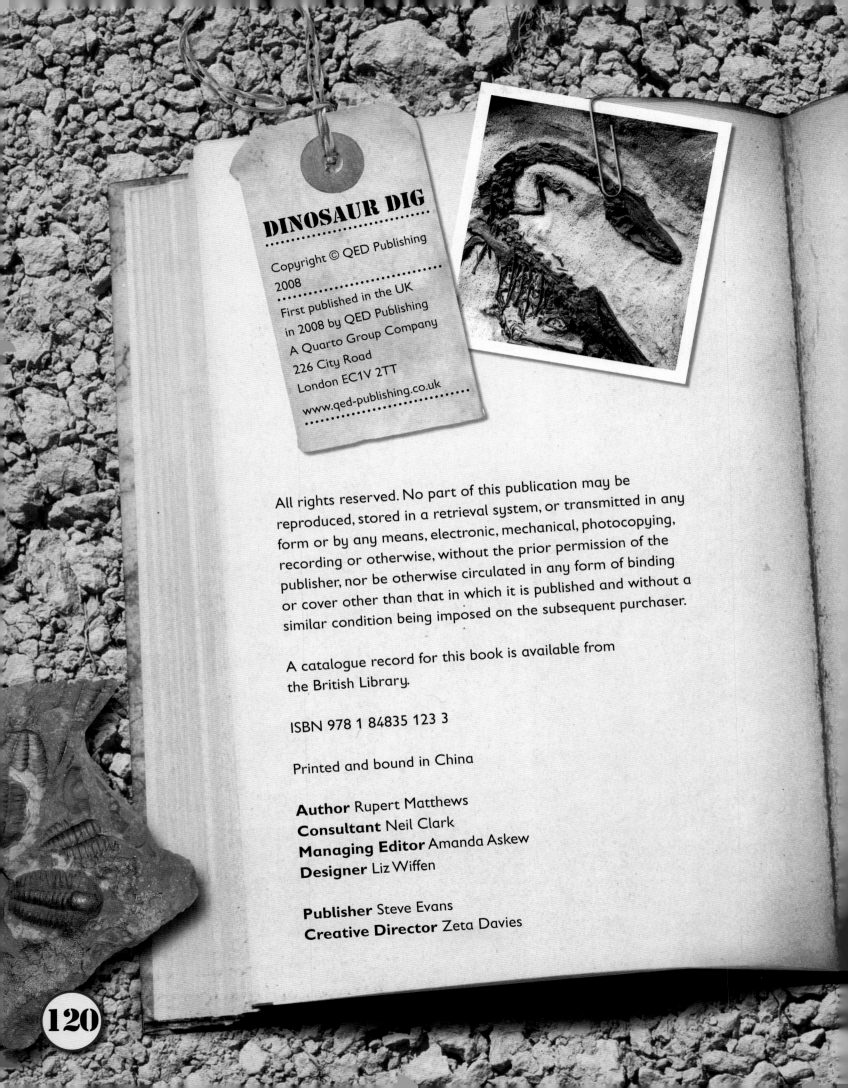

DINOSAUR DIG

Copyright © QED Publishing 2008

First published in the UK in 2008 by QED Publishing

A Quarto Group Company
226 City Road
London EC1V 2TT
www.qed-publishing.co.uk

A catalogue record for this book is available from the British Library.

ISBN 978 1 84835 123 3

Printed and bound in China

Author Rupert Matthews
Consultant Neil Clark
Managing Editor Amanda Askew
Designer Liz Wiffen

Publisher Steve Evans
Creative Director Zeta Davies